5 PRINCIPLES TO ENCOURAGE EVANGELISM

SESSION 2

DR. AARON R. JONES
Foreword by Dr. Timothy M. Hill

Interfacing Evangelism and Discipleship

WORKBOOK

5 Principles to Encourage Evangelism

Dr. Aaron R. Jones

Interfacing Evangelism and Discipleship Workbook

5 Principles to Encourage Evangelism

Copyright © 2018 by Dr. Aaron R. Jones

Printed in the United States of America

Published by Kingdom Publishing, LLC, Odenton, MD 21113

All rights reserved. No part of this book may be reproduced or transmitted in any form or by any means, electronic or mechanical, including photocopying, recording or by any information storage and retrieval system without written permission from the author, except for the inclusion of brief quotations in a review.

All scripture quotations are from the King James Version of the Bible. Thomas Nelson Publishers, Nashville: Thomas Nelson, Inc. 1972

Editor: Sharon D. Jones

Graphic Designer: Janell McIlwain – JM Virtual Concepts

                Tiara Smith

ISBN 978-1-947741-17-1

Table of Contents

Interfacing Evangelism and Discipleship SESSIONS 1

Foreword 2

Introduction 3

Principle #1 **The Last Day Mentality (2 Timothy 3:1-5)** 4

Principle #2 **The Blood on Our Hands (Ezekiel 3:17-19)** 10

Principle #3 **Desperate for One (Luke 15:3-7)** 14

Principle #4 **The Harvest is Ready! (Matthew 9:37, 38)** 18

Principle #5 **Redeem the Time (Ephesians 5:16, 18)** 23

About the Author 27

Contact Page 29

Interfacing Evangelism and Discipleship
SESSIONS

Session 1—**Introduction and Philosophy**

Session 2—**5 Principles to Encourage Evangelism**

Session 3—**Components of Evangelism**

Session 4—**Bait for Evangelism**

Session 5—**Methodology of Evangelism**

Session 6—**Church Planting Produces Evangelism and Discipleship**

Session 7—**Babes in Christ**

Session 8—**Components of Discipleship**

Session 9—**Evangelism and Discipleship Plan**

Session 10—**Spirit of Forgiveness**

Foreword

When God calls a man of faith and fortitude to a specific purpose in the building of His Kingdom, He uses an individual like Dr. Aaron Jones.

Feeling the urgency of the hour, Dr. Jones has shaped his participation in the FINISH Commitment by emphasizing the merging of evangelism and discipleship strategies to assist churches and individuals in their quests to effectively reach the lost. As Senior Pastor of New Hope Church of God, he is well-aware of what it takes to affect the Great Commission of our Lord.

Dr. Jones' desire is to instruct others on how to deliberately make an impact on winning souls and then discipling them for powerful Christian service. His all-inclusive approach will intrigue and provide the impetus for those willing to pursue the heart of God.

Interfacing Evangelism and Discipleship will change the course of your outreach!

Dr. Timothy M. Hill
General Overseer
Church of God, Cleveland, Tennessee

Introduction

The following principles should awake the spirit-man in all believers. This awakening should cause believers to reach the lost at any cost.

_____
_____
_____
_____
_____
_____

These 5 principles are meant to encourage and empower believers to evangelize.

_____
_____
_____
_____
_____
_____
_____

Principle #1

The Last Day Mentality[1] (2 Timothy 3:1-5)

---

[1] Jones, Aaron R., *The Soul Initiative for Eternity,* Kingdom Kaught Publishing, LLC, Denton, Maryland ©2015.

Principle #1

The Last Day Mentality

2 Timothy 3:1-5

"This know also, that in the last days perilous times shall come. For men shall be lovers of their own selves, covetous, boasters, proud, blasphemers, disobedient to parents, unthankful, unholy, without natural affection, trucebreakers, false accusers, incontinent, fierce, despisers of those that are good, Traitors, heady, highminded, lovers of pleasures more than lovers of God; Having a form of godliness, but denying the power thereof: from such turn away."

_____
_____
_____
_____
_____
_____
_____

- *Men shall be lovers of themselves.*

- *Man is covetous.*

- *Man is proud.*

- *Man is unthankful.*

- *Man is unholy.*

- *Man loves pleasure more than God.*

- *Man has a form of godliness but denies the power of God.*

Additional Notes

Principle #2

The Blood on Our Hands

(Ezekiel 3:17-19)

Principle #2

The Blood on Our Hands

Ezekiel 3:17-19

"Son of man, I have made thee a watchman unto the house of Israel: therefore hear the word at my mouth, and give them warning from me. When I say unto the wicked, Thou shalt surely die; and thou givest him not warning, nor speakest to warn the wicked from his wicked way, to save his life; the same wicked man shall die in his iniquity; but his blood will I require at thine hand. "Yet if thou warn the wicked, and he turn not from his wickedness, nor from his wicked way, he shall die in his iniquity; but thou hast delivered thy soul."

The Watchman

_____

_____

_____

The Warning

The Wicked

Additional Notes

Principle #3

Desperate for One
(Luke 15:3-7)

Principle #3

Desperate for One

Luke 15:3-7

"And he spake this parable unto them, saying, What man of you, having an hundred sheep, if he lose one of them, doth not leave the ninety and nine in the wilderness, and go after that which is lost, until he find it? And when he hath found it, he layeth it on his shoulders, rejoicing. And when he cometh home, he calleth together his friends and neighbours, saying unto them, Rejoice with me; for I have found my sheep which was lost. I say unto you, that likewise joy shall be in heaven over one sinner that repenteth, more than over ninety and nine just persons, which need no repentance."

The One

_____
_____
_____
_____

The Ninety-Nine

_____
_____
_____
_____

The Joy

_____
_____
_____
_____

Additional Notes

Principle #4

The Harvest is Ready! (Matthew 9:37, 38)

Principle #4

The Harvest is Ready!

Matthew 9:37, 38

Then saith he unto his disciples, "The harvest truly is plenteous, but the labourers are few; Pray ye therefore the Lord of the harvest, that he will send forth labourers into his harvest."

_____

_____

_____

_____

_____

_____

_____

- Help (Matthew 5:35, 36)

_____

_____

_____

_____

- Love (Luke 19:10)

_____

_____

_____

_____

- Pray (Romans 10:1)

_____

_____

_____

_____

Principle #4 The Harvest is Ready! (Matthew 9:37, 38)

- Send (Acts 13:2)

_____
_____
_____
_____
_____

- Go (Isaiah 6:8)

_____
_____
_____
_____
_____

Additional Notes

Principle #5

Redeem the Time (Ephesians 5:16, 18)

Principle #5

Redeem the Time

Ephesians 5:15-16

"See then that ye walk circumspectly, not as fools, but as wise, redeeming the time, because the days are evil."

Principle #5 Redeem the Time (Ephesians 5:16, 18)

_____
_____
_____
_____
_____
_____
_____
_____

- Will you no longer be judgmental and reach that wounded soul?

- Will you leave that soul to die?

- Will you redeem the time and help him/her know Jesus?

Additional Notes

❖❖❖❖❖

About the Author

DR. AARON R. JONES serves as Senior Pastor of New Hope Church of God. Under his pastorate is New Hope Kiddie Kollege, Inc (Daycare) and New Hope Community Outreach Services, Inc. Dr. Jones also oversees New Hope Church of God Ghana (2 churches) and New Hope Church of God Uganda (3 churches).

Dr. Jones is an Ordained Bishop with the Church of God denomination and is the DELMARVA-DC District Overseer (16 churches). Dr. Jones serves on DELMARVA-DC's Regional Council, Ministerial Internship Program Board, Urban Ministry Committee, Finance Committee, and Chaplain's Board. He also serves on both the Church of God's International and DELMARVA-DC Ministry to the Military Board. In his local community, Dr. Jones serves as a Chaplain for the Charles County Sheriff Department. He also serves as Board Secretary for the United Ministers Coalition of Southern Maryland, Inc.

Being obedient to 2 Timothy 2:15, "Study to show thyself approved…," Dr. Jones received a Doctorate in Theology and Pastoral Counseling from Life Christian University and a Doctorate in Christian Counseling from American Christian College and Seminary. He is a certified Pastoral Counselor with the International Association of Christian Counseling Professionals. He is a Life and Pastoral Coach. He is the former Executive Vice President of the National Bible College and Seminary in Fort Washington, Maryland.

Dr. Jones has published ten books and a soul-wining project that provide a biblical foundation for Christian doctrine and discipline. He has recorded a CD entitled, Peace in the Storm. He is the founder and owner of God's Comfort Ministries, LLC, which provides Christian literature, evangelism training, and spiritual guidance. He has appeared live on TCT Network; WATC-TV's Atlanta Live; Babbie's House (hosted by CCM artist Babbie Mason); and In Concert Today on DCTV. He has done radio interviews with Radio One's WYCB's program; The Praise Fest Show; and online with Total Prayze. He was featured on the cover of Change Gospel Magazine and interviewed on Promoting Purpose Magazine.

Dr. Jones not only serves God, but his country as well. He has served over 20 years in the Armed Forces. He is a retired Chaplain with the Army National Guard. He participated in both Operation Noble Eagle (2003) and Operation Iraqi Freedom III (2005).

Dr. Jones is happily married to the former Sharon Russell. He sincerely believes without her love, support, and encouragement, many of his goals would not have been accomplished.

Contact Page

Mailing Address: 150 Post Office Road #1079
Waldorf, Maryland 20604

Website: www.godscomfort.net

Email: drjones@godscomfortmin.net

Facebook: God's Comfort Ministries

Twitter: @GodsComfort_Min

Instagram: @godscomfort_min

GOD'S COMFORT MINISTRIES

God's Comfort Ministries (GCM) provides practical Christian books, teachings, trainings, and coaching to new converts and seasoned believers. GCM provides understanding of the doctrinal principles of the Bible.

Services Provided

Pastoral and Life Coaching

Evangelism and Discipleship Training

Spiritual Guidance

New Author Consultation

Christian Literature

www.ingramcontent.com/pod-product-compliance
Lightning Source LLC
Chambersburg PA
CBHW081358080526
44588CB00016B/2530